© KEEP GOING with a Smile
BY SANDEEP RAVIDUTT SHARMA

**Copyright © 2018
by Sandeep Ravidutt Sharma**

All rights reserved. No part of this book may be reproduced or transmitted in any form or by any means without written permission from the author.

If you have further questions, contact on

**Phone: +919969256731
Email: sandeepraviduttsharma@gmail.com**

© **KEEP GOING with a Smile**
BY SANDEEP RAVIDUTT SHARMA

Dedication

This book is dedicated to **Shiva Shakti** - the epitome of love. Lord Shiva is pure consciousness symbolising the masculine principle. Goddess Shakti symbolises the active feminine energy of Shiva and is synonymously identified with **Tripura Sundari, Sati** or **Parvati**. These primal principles are also called as PURUSHA representing consciousness and PRAKRITI denoting the nature. Shiva and Shakti are manifestations of the all-in-one divine consciousness. Shiva is the paternal love of God that gives us consciousness, knowledge and clarity. Shakti is the motherly love of God that showers warmth and care and ensures our protection. Shiva and Shakti exist within each of us as the masculine and feminine energy.

To please **Shiva Shakti** praying for the well being, love, happiness, strength, positive energy and success of my readers in their life, i hereby recite the following mantra...

"Sarva Mangala Mangalye Shive Sarvartha Sadhike Sharanye Tryambake Gauri Narayani Namostute"

> **© KEEP GOING with a Smile**
> BY SANDEEP RAVIDUTT SHARMA

Table of Contents

Foreword IV
KEEP GOING with a Smile.. 1

© **KEEP GOING with a Smile**
BY SANDEEP RAVIDUTT SHARMA

Foreword

This book provides you with a list of **100** quotes and thoughts about life, churned out by my mind with the consciousness, grace and energy of **Shiva Shakti**.

I'm sure if you keep reading, referring and sharing these thoughts and quotes about life, you will draw motivation and inspiration. These quotes can reiterate your commitment and boost your efforts in moving forward with determination.

"Don't bother about the Twist and Turns of life. Keep Going with a Smile."

I sincerely hope, you will find this book amazing, interesting, rejuvenating, unique and a constant source of Inspiration.

Thank You and Happy Reading.

© **KEEP GOING with a Smile**
BY SANDEEP RAVIDUTT SHARMA

KEEP GOING
with a Smile

© **KEEP GOING with a Smile**
BY SANDEEP RAVIDUTT SHARMA

Change with time or it will change you forever.

© **KEEP GOING with a Smile**
BY SANDEEP RAVIDUTT SHARMA

Why fear about the past or future, when you are in love with the present. Present cannot ditch you if you hold it firmly and live with it.

Raise your voice if you have decided to lend it for a noble cause. Make sure your voice is heard till the last row in an assembly.

© **KEEP GOING with a Smile**
BY SANDEEP RAVIDUTT SHARMA

Don't bother about thousands of thorns placed in your life path. You better focus on your walk and aim to reach the destination.

© **KEEP GOING with a Smile**
BY SANDEEP RAVIDUTT SHARMA

Don't expect to accelerate all the time when you drive on the life pathway.

Don't build castle in the air. Instead build a bridge on the ground and help people to connect.

> © **KEEP GOING with a Smile**
> BY SANDEEP RAVIDUTT SHARMA

At least during crisis we should co-operate and not compete with each other.

> *Inspiration is all around, all you need is clarity of thought and good intentions to seek it.*

Escape from the clutches of worries by following the path of happiness which guarantees welfare of all. Happiness path is laid for those who strongly visualise to be in a happy state. For a strong visualization you need to focus on what you want and how. Once you do this start believing that you have already got what you wanted. Realisation of happiness is quite close.

People may come in or go out of your life. You may remember only those who touched your heart and soul.

> © **KEEP GOING with a Smile**
> BY SANDEEP RAVIDUTT SHARMA

Life path may be full of thorns or flowers. Keep Going is the mantra to reach your destination. Cheer up. It's a long way to go.

© **KEEP GOING with a Smile**
BY SANDEEP RAVIDUTT SHARMA

Avoid living in the past at any cost.

Life path may appear to be serene all around and laid in an uneven way. It all depends on whether you keep going by enjoying the serene look or just want to focus on the path laid to avoid falling and reaching your destination. Life is more about the journey than the destination. Maintain balance while you walk.

Sun rises and bring lots of hope for everyone except darkness.

> © **KEEP GOING** with a Smile
> BY SANDEEP RAVIDUTT SHARMA

Don't build tunnels to live in but pass through the other end at the earliest.

Achievers shine even when they are no more. Achievers are not made in a day. Time grinds them and moulds them in a form which shines and is difficult to break.

Human without emotions is no human at all.

When you request something from someone and you use magical words 'please' or 'kindly'. Most of the time the delivery or the task completion is guaranteed. Words can seal or kill a deal.

If you keep using the word 'Sorry' without changing your own conduct and behaviour. Your words would lose their credibility forever.

Look beyond your own self and make a difference in the life of others.

Even a super sonic jet can't fly forever, it needs to rest in the parking bay. Same way, take a pause from your busy schedule, relax for a while and you are rejuvenated.

People overthrow leaders who get desperate to rule the world.

Waves cannot be curtailed because you have build a Sand castle on the beach. Waves will touch it's mark in a hurry and return back gently.

> © **KEEP GOING with a Smile**
> BY SANDEEP RAVIDUTT SHARMA

Turbulence loves going places and is always temporary. Keep Going with a smile and you win.

Everyone considers self to be the best. But only the best ones remember that only efforts make them the best.

> © **KEEP GOING with a Smile**
> BY SANDEEP RAVIDUTT SHARMA

Compare yourself or others not with the intention to get demotivated or put someone down but to excel further.

© **KEEP GOING with a Smile**
BY SANDEEP RAVIDUTT SHARMA

Nature discards itself and make attempt to regenerate.

Most of the time we all are alone. Friends and family members can give you company only for certain distance. Make attempt to connect with the nature and the creator. God loves all.

Find ME time when you are alone and can talk to your own self.

Today is my day. I'm here to win. No one can stop me from winning.

Conditional love is no love at all. It's a deal.

Don't fast when it's time to feast.

Life path is hardly straight except when you are near your destination. Enjoy the zig zag journey even if you fall sometime as it would teach lesson for your life.

When God auctions. Stake your claim on righteousness, kindness, love, peace, forgiveness and patience.

Every time you blame someone else for your failure, you are climbing down on the success ladder.

There is nothing called as extra time. Whatever you intend to do, you need to do it in the time allotted by the creator. You don't know when the alarm bell will ring and time up is declared. Live Now. Discuss tomorrow if it comes.

Innovation never ends and is the key to human progress.

When failure meets persistent efforts, Success is close by.

No one is perfect in this world. Crave for perfection but don't wait for perfection. Pursuing perfection can lead to excellence

When you resist change, the real problem starts. Accept change and resist oppression of any kind.

Keep Going even when you have achieved something because life never stops.

> © **KEEP GOING with a Smile**
> BY SANDEEP RAVIDUTT SHARMA

To walk you don't have to wait for the right inspiration. All you need is your feet and eyes set on the life path.

© **KEEP GOING with a Smile**
BY SANDEEP RAVIDUTT SHARMA

Don't bother about the world.
Celebrate each moment.

Most of us are losing the present due to bothering too much about the future.

Sun rays right in the morning is refreshing and reassuring of your continued existence. Thanks to Sun God for bringing life to the fore.

Don't bother too much about life after death, when you have so much to do in the current life.

Don't bother too much about what the world thinks about you. What matters is about your self image.

Make attempt to find purpose of your life.

Life lessons never end.

Sometimes when you see the path laid, the destination seems to be near. It's only when you actually walk and reach the seemingly end point, realisation dawns on you about your short sightedness and location of the goal post. Focus on your next step and you will find goal post coming nearer.

Every second counts for your success. But don't just spend time in counting each second.

Rear mirror can only give you a hint of what may cross your path. You can't simply depend on it to move forward.

Inspire the world with your words and deeds.

If you have flood of questions, it means you are making attempt to learn and understand.

Things or people who appealed from a distance may not be beautiful in the real world when brought closer. Look and crave for the beauty of the mind and heart.

When no one seems to be in your favour then don't lose heart, the creator of all would always protect you. Have faith.

People in our lives either touch or torch our hearts. It all depends on how do you react in either case. Forgive those who torch. Embrace those who touch. Forget about those who neither touch nor torch. They don't exist for you.

Sometimes when you are not able to judge what is right or wrong, have faith and simply leave the decision to the almighty God. Whatever he decides is always good for you.

© **KEEP GOING with a Smile**
BY SANDEEP RAVIDUTT SHARMA

Keep Smiling and Shining.

No treasure is as valuable as your character.

> © **KEEP GOING with a Smile**
> BY SANDEEP RAVIDUTT SHARMA

Live your dreams now.

Sometimes when you are disturbed, you may start feeling that world is not enough. Remind yourself that the world is within your own heart under the protection of Supreme Soul. Whose realm is limitless.

Sometimes you wait for months and years to perform for a minute on the life stage. Dream, Efforts and Patience are your constant companion.

Wave do not expect to live forever. Despite this the wave is eager to touch the shore.

No one knows you better than your own self. Avoid playing hide and seek, explore and have faith in your own ability.

Competition is a man made phenomenon. Healthy competition ensures the best. No competition many a times kills the spirit to innovate.

Accumulate wealth to spend and not to rust.

© **KEEP GOING with a Smile**
BY SANDEEP RAVIDUTT SHARMA

Draw inspiration from people, places and thoughts. Keep Going...

In the classroom of life not everything can be taught, time gives you number of opportunity to learn certain things or facts on your own. So get ready to learn how to cross thorny paths laid for you to reach your destiny.

Even a beggar can give blessings then how come one say that I don't have anything to give. Kind words coming out of one's heart are unlimited.

Achievers are those who start with a single step forward focusing on their performance not just one but each of them. These are not the guys made of metal but are the simpler ones like most of us. Extra efforts in mission mode separates extraordinary from ordinary beings.

Don't miss any opportunity to celebrate. Share happiness and joy in your journey of life.

Reforms should start from your own door. When you put into practice what you have learned and preach, life would bloom.

© **KEEP GOING with a Smile**
BY SANDEEP RAVIDUTT SHARMA

Waves and Wind never moves forward in silence.

© **KEEP GOING with a Smile**
BY SANDEEP RAVIDUTT SHARMA

There is no way you can press a button and erase your depressing memories. Living in the present is the only way forward to forget them.

Most of the time, Old and New coexist. Old slowly fades away into new and New becomes old with passage of time.

It's easy to do things which you like and feel happy. In the opposite case it is important how you condition your mind to do things more joyfully even when you dislike them and it has come your way. Your approach counts more when things don't appear the way you want.

Wonderful thoughts refreshes our mind. Transform these thoughts into wonderful reality.

Most of us including yours truly get attracted to Gold easily. Gold need not be just metallic. It can be Golden Sun Shine, Golden moments or Golden words.

© **KEEP GOING with a Smile**
BY SANDEEP RAVIDUTT SHARMA

Accompany happiness by sticking to positive thoughts.

© **KEEP GOING with a Smile**
BY SANDEEP RAVIDUTT SHARMA

Keep Going. Whether you are on the bridge or on the ground. Remember to keep an eye on your destination.

Find out what makes you run from problems and how can you stay put to resolve forever.

Compare today with yesterday and you know the progress achieved.

Even a fake smile is better than a permanent frown.

> © **KEEP GOING with a Smile**
> BY SANDEEP RAVIDUTT SHARMA

Life never gets completed with only happiness. Sorrow waits for you to at least have a glimpse. Happiness and Sorrow follow each other quite often. Your attitude and behaviour decides how long each stays.

© **KEEP GOING with a Smile**
BY SANDEEP RAVIDUTT SHARMA

Every time you smile, return gift in the form of another smile is guaranteed

© **KEEP GOING with a Smile**
BY SANDEEP RAVIDUTT SHARMA

Fill and feel the light of kindness and love in your life.

No one remembers smooth ride. Challenging rides become memories.

Reality takes over everything. Sometimes you lose and many a times you gain provided you have constantly monitored the situation and implemented adjustments wherever and whenever required in an ethical way.

When you buy a gift and give it to someone, it's a message of likeness and love for the other person. You generally don't gift to your enemies but try doing it and you may even win your enemy.

Sun rises and sets every day is our belief for ages but the fact is Sun always glows while the perspective of earth changes every minute and it seems Sun is drifting from east to west.

Watch the world with your eyes and binoculars. Feel the world with your heart and happiness fills in soon.

Don't try to wear shoes that won't fit your size. You would lose on your money, trouble your leg and ultimately affect your style. Same way do things which you can manage and matches with your level of knowledge and expertise.

To wish it doesn't cost a penny but to fulfill it would at least need a drop of your sweat.

Achievers are the one who don't always depend on any kind of external motivation. Self motivation is in their blood.

Living in isolation is advisable only for those who are fed with up staying in limelight for most of their life.

© **KEEP GOING with a Smile**
BY SANDEEP RAVIDUTT SHARMA

Don't turn your mind into a machine else you will need frequent maintenance.

It's strange to understand why we get more than what we deserve sometimes, while at other times it's in the reverse order. Acceptability with gratitude is the key to happiness in both the cases.

Amazing world awaits to cheer. You are to win and share happiness.

Keep Going even when the choice is not clear. At least you will reach somewhere and not just remain frozen in one place.

www.ingramcontent.com/pod-product-compliance
Lightning Source LLC
Chambersburg PA
CBHW031438210526
45464CB00005B/2258